The Everyday Allergy Free Cookbook

Enjoy Amazing, Easy Recipes without Dairy, Gluten, Soy, Eggs, Fish, Shellfish, Nuts, Fruits or Spices

Comfortable Allergen-Friendly Cooking for Kids and Adults

Tiffany Shelton

Disclaimer

The recipes and information in this book are provided for educational purposes only. Please always consult a licensed professional before making changes to your lifestyle or diet. The author and publisher shall have neither liability nor responsibility to anyone with respect to any loss or damage caused or alleged to be caused directly or indirectly by the information contained in this book. All trademarks and brands within this book are for clarifying purposes only and are owned by the owners themselves, not affiliated with this document.

Images from shutterstock.com

CONTENTS

INTRODUCTION

Every person suffering from allergies has a history of its occurrence. Food allergies are observed in millions of American children. Different types of allergies are becoming more common in many other countries. Scientists have only partially described the process of occurrence of an allergic reaction yet. So, it is still unclear why food causes allergies. But it is absolutely clear that allergic people should avoid foods that cause an allergic reaction. Many people believe healthy food without allergens is not tasty and impossible to eat for pleasure. This is not the case. You can eat tasty food without breaking the rules that your allergy dictates to you.

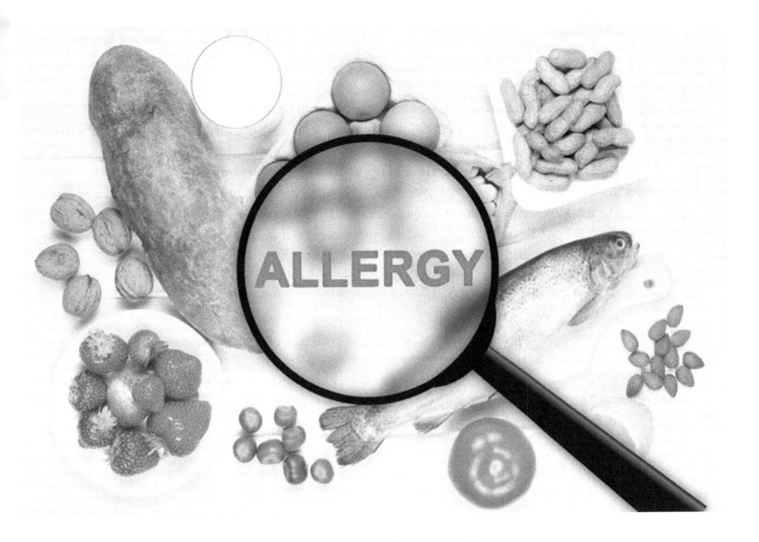

Causes of Allergic Reactions

Hereditary predisposition. Dermatologists and allergists are increasingly convinced that the tendency to allergic reactions is inherited. In this case, not allergic diseases are inherited, but only a predisposition to them

Irrational food. Excessive love for chocolate or citrus can even cause an allergic reaction in a healthy body

Gastrointestinal diseases create a fertile ground for allergies

Artificial feeding of infant increases the risk of developing an allergy many times.

Symptoms

Symptoms of food allergy include:

- Tingling in the mouth and swelling of the lips;
- Indigestion;
- Labored breathing;
- Reddening of the skin, itching, and hives;
- Distraction, drowsiness.

How to Avoid or Minimize the Manifestation of Allergic Reactions

✓ The abundance of easily absorbable carbohydrates (sugar, honey, confectionery) creates favorable conditions for the development of allergies

✓ In case when signs of allergies have begun to recur, try to carefully analyze your diet to help the specialist determine which products are dangerous for you and prescribe the necessary treatment. Try to record for 2-3 weeks all that you have eaten in a day, not forgetting to note the amount and method of cooking. Regularly note the time of appearance and the nature of the allergic reaction

✓ Pay attention to food what you eat with pleasure, and what you do not like. The unconscious reaction often suggests what exactly serves as a food allergen. Just try to listen to your inner voice, do not force yourself to eat a dish that you do not like, just because it is healthy.

✓ During baking, stewing and boiling vegetables and fruits, their allergenic activity is significantly reduced. For example, boiled or stewed carrots are less likely to cause allergies than raw ones. If you are allergic to fresh apples, replace them with stewed apples. Often the cause of allergic reactions is the skin of the fruit, try to peel it

✓ The most allergenic are fat and fried meat dishes, as well as poultry, pork, and lamb. Since different varieties of meat differ in their protein composition, when you are allergic, for example, to pork, you can eat beef or lamb. In case you need to boil broth to make soup, place the meat in cold water - most of the proteins that cause an allergic reaction will go in it. Drain the first broth after boiling

✓ If you are sensitive to cow's milk, you can replace it with lactic acid products, for example, yogurt or with dairy-free milk

Remember to be a little bit more attentive to the things you eat. Enjoy your meal and enjoy your life!

Food to Avoid

There are a lot of theories about the reasons for allergies. However, none have been definitively proven. An allergy is a hypersensitivity reaction that triggers specific immune mechanisms. Allergens are substances which cause allergies. About 6-8% of children aged from one to three years have an allergy to certain foods. In the country, about 5% of the population suffers from food allergies. Besides this, the problem touches a lot of other people who are not allergic persons, but they need to take care of their relatives and friends. So, let's take a look at the most common types of allergies.

Dairy
Usually, cow's milk allergy has quite good predictions. Most of the children get rid of it before they reach school age. Infants who have had negative test results are often allowed to resume milk intake after half a year or a year. It is not known how many adults suffer from milk allergies, but it is assumed that this number does not constitute more than one percent of the population. Nevertheless, there is a multitude of protein in cow's milk and dairy products. Since the chemical composition of goat's and cow's milk is different, replacing cow's milk with goat's milk may help. If you are allergic to both cow's and goat's milk, you should avoid all foods containing milk and dairy products, such as butter, cottage cheese, and ice-cream. In case of dairy allergy, it is necessary to take care of sufficient intake of calcium, iodine, and vitamin B.

Gluten
Mainly based in cereals - wheat, rye, barley. These are also used for the preparation of many other products, in particular, sauces (mayonnaise and ketchup) and dressings, ready-made soups and other semi-finished products, sweets and chocolate, dairy products and beer. For allergy sufferers, not only are

foods with a clear presence of gluten dangerous, but also those with a hidden gluten content, including canned food, sausages, meat and fish semi-finished products, instant noodles, mashed potatoes, bouillon cubes, chips, soy sauce, ketchup, processed cheese curds, curd pastes, yoghurts, chocolates, a variety of caramel, and ice cream.

Soy

Since soy protein is widely used in the production of sausages and confections, hamburgers, pizza, bread, and other bakery products. So, it goes without saying that people who are allergic to soy protein should be very careful. Soybean oil, in contrast, does not cause allergies. The only way to combat soybean allergy is to completely eliminate foods containing soy protein from the diet. In any case, there is a very big amount of soy-free food. Soy protein is absent in products made from pure milk, eggs, meat, fish, crustaceans and mollusks, fruits, nuts, vegetable oil or vegetables.

Eggs

This type of allergy usually begins in early childhood. Most of the allergens in the egg are in the protein, but egg yolk can also be problematic. Egg allergy is more common among children than adults. The majority of egg allergy disappears with age, but for some people, it persists in adult life too. Such items as egg white, yolk, egg powder can indicate the egg content in food. Sometimes such names as albumin or egg lysozymes can also indicate the presence of egg proteins in food. Among the products that often contain an egg are cakes, cookies, seasonings, sauces, mayonnaise and salads with its content, mustard, spaghetti, pasta, waffles, pancakes, sweets, breadcrumbs, and casseroles.

Nuts

People with nut allergies need to be especially careful and attentively read the labels of the products they buy. Nuts mean hazelnuts, cashews, pistachios, walnuts, pecans, almonds. From a biological point of view, peanuts, or groundnuts, is not a nut but belongs to the family of leguminous. Therefore, some people who are allergic to peanuts also exhibit sensitivity or allergic symptoms when eating leguminous plants: green peas, soybeans, beans, lupine, and lentils. Nut-based foods also include nougat, nut cream, sugar-roasted almonds, biscuit fillers, and almond base for cakes. Other products that often contain nuts include cakes, biscuits, breakfast mixes, salads, bread, desserts, chocolate, ice cream, pesto, and some foreign dishes such as Asian cuisine.

Fish

An allergy of this kind is usually to finned fish. A reaction can occur from eating or touching fish or eating something that contains fish byproducts. People allergic to fish should avoid not only seafood but also some convenience foods contain fish or fish products. For instance, liver pate, which contains anchovies, as well as tapenades, Caesar salad dressing, and manchester sauce. Crab salad can contain fish, and crab sticks are made from fish, not from marine crustaceans. Oyster or fish sauce is made from fish and sea cranberries, which can also cause allergic exposure.

Shellfish

Allergy to shellfish can be more serious than many other allergies and can last for a lifetime. People who have an allergic reaction to shellfish, most often, react to all the shellfish, not just to their particular species. It is not very difficult to avoid shellfish in the diet, moreover, it does not lead to the loss of nutrients. The main shellfish causing an allergic reaction are: snails, octopuses and mussels. There are also cross-reactions between species. Note that their shells can be used as colorants. In addition, the cure for joint pain, glucosamine, is made from the shells, which can also lead to an allergic reaction. It should also be noted that there is no connection between allergy to fish and allergy to shellfish.

Vegetables/Fruits

Jams, juices, boiled, and frozen vegetables don't usually cause an allergic reaction. Apricots, bananas, kiwi, apples, peaches, and exotic fruits (like mango, papaya, carambola) are the most common allergens among fruits. For vegetables, the most dangerous are paprika, turnips, carrots, beets, and onions.

Spices

Spice allergy is a rare occurrence, but the risk of its presence is increased if you are allergic to pollen. This is called cross allergy. Herbs often contain large amounts of essential oils that can cause skin rashes. You may also have a reaction to the protein in spices. Usually, if you are allergic to any kind of spices. Even when its symptoms are mild, you shouldn't completely exclude the possibility of developing more serious problems. Curry, ginger, cinnamon, pepper, coriander, and cumin are the most common allergic reaction inducing spices.

How to Replace

Dairy substitutes

Hypoallergenic milk replacer is recommended for young children, which can be purchased at the pharmacy. Adults can use such milk replacers as rice milk, oat milk, coconut milk, etc. The amount of calcium contained in these foods corresponds to the calcium content in cow's milk, but these drinks often contain less protein and nutrients. Milk substitutes purchased in a pharmacy can be used in the cooking of most dishes. Soy milk, rice milk or coconut milk also may be used. Although, almost all the following products are available in a dairy-free version - margarine, sour cream, yogurt, ice cream, and cream substitutes based on soy, rice or oats.

Gluten substitutes

Grains such as corn, rice, buckwheat, millet, quinoa, sorghum, and millet are good substitutes for wheat, rye, and barley. Many dairy-allergic people can also eat gluten-free oats without any allergic reactions. Furthermore, very suitable are special gluten-free foods: flour mixes, pasta, biscuits, crispbread, and breakfast cereal mixes. Some of them contain wheat starch, but the amount of protein in it is so insignificant that for most people with allergies this will not be a problem. Gluten-free foods can be found in stores with a wide range of products, as well as in specialized healthy-food stores. Some bakeries sell gluten-free pastries. Gluten-free products, such as gluten-free bread and cereal mixes, are often based on rice, corn, potato or wheat starch.

Soy substitutes

Many people with soy-allergy react only to cold soy drinks and soy yogurt. They, as a rule, may not take into account the presence of soy in mixed products, since most of the baked goods, meat, and other products with soy are consumed in a heated way and do not pose a danger. In addition, in most cases, people with allergies to soy is not contraindicated in eating soy oil. In the process of oil production, the proteins that cause allergic reactions to disappear. The results of the analysis of soy oils show the absence of soy protein in some of them.

Eggs substitutes

An egg is a nutrient-rich product, but it is not essential for a healthy diet. Likewise, eggs have properties that are important for making good bakery products. Egg substitutes can be found in stores, such as "No Egg" and "Egg Replacer", which have similar binding and other properties required for baking, but they differ in the composition of nutrients. In many cases, a good egg substitute can be obtained by increasing the amount of baking powder or soda. One egg can be replaced with one tablespoon of baking powder. You can get the same golden color of the dough as while using eggs, by adding 1-2 tablespoons of cornmeal. Moreover, the vast majority of pastry made from yeast dough, jelly, chocolate sauces, frozen juice, sorbet, fruits, and berries do not contain egg elements and are delightful desserts.

Nuts substitutes

A recent study shows that over 50% of people who are allergic to certain nuts can easily consume other nut culture. Since peanuts are more classified as legumes, the researchers noticed that almost no one who is allergic to peanuts was allergic to other types of nuts. Thus, while dermatological analysis may find that a person is allergic to nuts, this is not certain, especially if this person has never tried another kind of nuts. However, people with a nut allergy are advised to try potential allergens under doctor control.

Fish substitutes

People with fish allergy most often tolerate well to fish oil, since it is fairly well purified from protein. Due to the fact that fish is an important source of omega-3 fatty acids, it is important to take fish oil or other sources of omega-3 in cases of allergy to fish. In addition, fish is an important source of iodine and selenium. The body's need for iodine can be satisfied through the consumption of dairy products, while products from grains, meat and, especially, nuts are good sources of selenium.

Shellfish substitutes

Most people with shellfish allergy are not allergic to fish, so they can replace each other.

Vegetables/Fruits substitutes

Nowadays the most different fruits and vegetables are freely available, and allergies to vegetables and fruits are not very common. However, if an allergy to the product is manifested, you can try to replace one fruit with another. In addition, most fruits and vegetables no longer cause allergic reactions after heat treatment. So, just try to cook them.

Spices substitutes

Spices are one of those allergens with almost none substitution. But there is also good news - there are many spices in the world, and there will definitely be some without an allergic reaction! If an allergic reaction manifests itself in any spices, this does not mean that all spices should be excluded from the diet, you only need to consult with an allergist and make a menu that does not harm your health.

Main Rules of Healthy Snacks

If you want your snacks to be healthy and bring only benefits, try to follow these useful rules:

- Only snack 2-3 times per day.
- Remember that each snack should be smaller and fewer calories than the main meal.
- Healthy snacks should consist only of healthy natural products.
- Snack 2-3 hours between meals.

If you are a snacker, consider having 2 snacks per day: after breakfast or afternoon tea. In the first part of the day, it is better to eat carbohydrates. Fruits, smoothies, green smoothies, different cereals with fresh fruits which are not very sweet, but include a lot of water that is very healthy or fruit salads after which you will not feeling hunger, and there will not be dangerous for your figure. Make the second snack protein. Nuts or a glass of nut milk make for a satisfying snack before dinner.

Remember to drink water all throughout the day.

Eating by the clock, not by need, leads to eating disorders. Learn to listen to the body, because no one knows you best.

Remember that all heavy food (snacks included) is better to eat in the first half of the day. The best snacks are not from the shop, the best and the most healthy snacks are homemade. Therefore, believe me, it's pretty easy to make allergy- free snacks and treats at home and I will prove it. We all understand that only one right way to get rid of every allergy is to stop contact with its source. For this purpose, I have prepared for your variety of recipes for every day, so that you can indulge yourself with goodies and not darken your life with thoughts about allergies. That is not an illness . Let's get rid of all in the same key. Only adjust your lifestyle a bit and enjoy this amazing world.

Measurement Conversions for Cooking Outside the United States

The measurements in this book may be confusing to those of you using the metric system. Here is a list of some of the ingredients In this book converted to grams. I have included a couple of other hours that you might use to substitute, as well.

- 1 cup white nee flour = 98 grams
- 1 cup Bob's Red Mill Gluten-Free All-Purpose Flour = 151 grams
- 1 cup garbanzo flour = 115 grams
- 1 cup potato starch = 174 grams
- 1 cup granulated sugar = 198 grams
- 1 cup shortening = 190 grams
- 1 cup packed dark brown sugar = 240 grams
- 1 cup packed light brown sugar = 215 grams

There are so many great gluten-free flours on the market, that rather than discuss all of them individually in the substitutions section, I thought it might be more helpful to give you a list of these flours and their weights so that you can substitute them interchangeably If you are outside the United States, I ounce is equal to 28 grams.

- 1 cup superfine white rice flour = 3.5 ounces
- 1 cup sorghum flour = 3.9 ounces
- 1 cup millet flour = 3.9 ounces
- 1 cup Bob s Red Mill Gluten-Free All-Purpose Flour = 5.4 ounces
- 1 cup potato starch = 6.2 ounces
- 1 cup potato flour = 6.2 ounces
- 1 cup Quinoa flour = 3.4 ounces
- 1 cup garbanzo flour = 4.1 ounces
- 1 cup tapioca starch = 3.7 ounces
- 1 cup buckwheat flour = 44 ounces

Myths And Facts About Allergies

Myth 1: "Food allergies are very common."

25% of people in the world think that they are allergic to certain food. But studies show that only 6% of children and 1-2% of adults suffer from food allergies.

Myth 2: "The most common allergies are to strawberries and tomatoes."

Babies and young children are most often allergic to milk, eggs, wheat, soy products, and peanuts. Older children and adults tend to be allergic to peanuts, nuts (such as walnuts, almonds, and cashews), fish, and shellfish.

Myth 3: "Adults are allergic to milk."

Many adults have trouble digesting carbohydrates in milk. This is called lactose intolerance. And this is not technically an allergy.

Myth 4: "Has an allergy started? You will live with it forever."

Allergies to milk, eggs, soy, and wheat usually stop in adulthood. However, allergies to nuts, fish, and shellfish rarely pass.

Fact 1: "Allergy is not a disease."

In spite of the fact of a whole complex of diagnostics of allergic reactions and drugs for relieving symptoms, allergy is not considered a disease. Experts stubbornly insist that the allergy is an acute (inadequate) body reaction to one or another environmental factor - an allergen.

Fact 2: "Firstborn children are more likely to suffer from allergic reactions than their younger brothers or sisters."

This fact was established by Japanese pediatricians on the basis of long-term observations. Scientists could not explain why it happens this way, no matter how hard they tried. So, they had to state a fact without any evidence.

Fact 3: "The most common allergy in recent years has become a food allergy."

The most common food allergen is a peanut.

Fact 4: "Not every reaction to food is an allergy."

Very often, people think that they suffer from allergy. However, they just have a food intolerance. Actually, these are two different things. One-fifth of the world's population suffers from food intolerance because of at least one product. To alleviate the symptoms, it is necessary to undergo a medical check-up and identify the real cause of the problem - is it really an allergy or food intolerance.

BREAKFAST

Strawberry Donuts

Prep time: 15 minutes

Cooking time: 14 minutes

Servings: 6

Suitable for: gluten-free dairy-free, soy-free, egg-free, fish-free, shellfish-free, nut-free, spices-free.

Nutrients per serving:

Carbohydrates – 64 g

Fat – 10 g

Protein – 3 g

Calories – 360

Ingredients:

- 1 cup gluten-free flour
- ½ cup of organic sugar
- ½ cup baking powder
- 6 tablespoons any non-dairy milk
- ¼ teaspoon salt
- 2 teaspoons strawberry juice
- ½ teaspoon white vinegar
- 1 teaspoon vanilla extract
- 2 tablespoons unsweetened applesauce
- ¼ cup vegan buttery spread melted

For the frosting:

- ½ confectionary sugar
- 2 tablespoons vegan buttery spread
- 6 chopped strawberry

Instructions:

1. Combine all the dry ingredients.
2. Add the melted buttery spread, any non-dairy milk, strawberry juice, unsweetened vanilla applesauce.
3. Spoon the batter into the donut pan. Smooth out the top of every donut.
4. Bake at 350 °F for 12-14 minutes.
5. Let cool for a few minutes. Place donuts onto a cookie sheet.
6. To make the frosting, whisk together the butter to soften, then add half powdered sugar. Sprinkle with non-dairy milk, continue to beat. Then add the remaining of the powdered sugar and continue to beat until creamy.
7. Frost chilled donuts, then top with sliced strawberries.

Chicken Sandwich

Prep time: 10 minutes

Cooking time: 20 minutes

Servings: 4

Suitable for: gluten-free, dairy-free, soy-free, egg-free, fish-free, shellfish-free, nut-free, vegetables/fruits free

Nutrients per serving:

Carbohydrates – 33 g

Fat – 31 g

Protein – 27 g

Calories – 555

Ingredients:

- 1 pound boneless, skinless chicken breasts
- ⅔ cup egg-free mayonnaise
- ¼ teaspoon pepper
- ¼ teaspoon salt
- 1½ teaspoons dill
- 8 slices gluten-free bread

Instructions:

1. Cook the chicken breasts in a pot of water for about 20 minutes.
2. Put cooked chicken breasts on a plate and let them cool.
3. Pulse the cooled, cooked chicken breasts in the food processor until the chicken is finely chopped.
4. Add the mayonnaise, salt, pepper, and dill. Stir.
5. Toast the gluten-free bread slices.
6. Spread the chicken salad on four slices of bread, then top with the other four slices of bread.

Dairy-Free Pancakes

Prep time: 10 minutes

Cooking time: 15 minutes

Servings: 8

Suitable for: gluten-free, dairy-free, soy-free, egg-free, fish-free, shellfish-free, nut-free, vegetables/fruits free, spices-free

Nutrients per serving:

Carbohydrates – 21 g

Fat – 6 g

Protein – 4 g

Calories – 159

Ingredients:

- ⅓ cup oats
- ¼ cup white flour
- 1 cup whole-spelled flour
- 1½ Tablespoons baking powder
- ¼ teaspoon salt
- ¼ cup vegan buttery spread, melted
- 2 Tablespoons brown sugar
- ¼ cup any non-dairy milk of your choice
- vegan buttery spread (for frying)

Instructions:

1. Process the oats in the food processor until a fine flour is formed.
2. Whisk together the whole-spelled flour, white flour, baking powder, ground oats, and salt.
3. Add the melted vegan buttery spread, non-dairy milk, and brown sugar and stir.
4. Place some buttery vegan spread in a frying pan over medium heat.
5. Fry both sides of pancakes for about 3-4 minutes.
6. Serve with buttery vegan spread on top.

Spicy Apple Cake

Prep time: 10 minutes

Cooking time: 38 minutes

Servings: 9

Suitable for: gluten-free, dairy-free, soy-free,
egg-free, fish-free, shellfish-free,
nut-free, vegetables/fruits free

Nutrients per serving:

Carbohydrates – 41 g

Fat – 9 g

Protein – 2 g

Calories – 249

Ingredients:

- 2 cups gluten-free flour blend
- 1 teaspoon baking soda
- ½ teaspoon baking powder
- ½ teaspoon salt
- ¼ teaspoon nutmeg
- 1¼ teaspoon cinnamon
- ½ teaspoon ginger
- ½ cup of sugar
- ½ cup coconut or brown sugar
- ⅓ cup canola oil
- 3 Tablespoons unsweetened apple sauce
- ¾ cup apple, peeled
- 1 teaspoon vanilla extract
- 1 teaspoon white vinegar
- ⅜ cup of water
- Powdered sugar to decorate

Instructions:

1. Preheat the oven to 350°F.
2. Combine the apple, applesauce, canola oil, water, vanilla extract, and vinegar.
3. Stir in the sugar, gluten free flour, baking powder, baking soda, salt, nutmeg, cinnamon, and ginger.
4. Put the dough in an 8x8 square pan lined with parchment paper.
5. Bake for 28-32 minutes.

Sweet Bread

Prep time: 10 minutes

Cooking time: 45 minutes

Servings: 8

Suitable for: gluten-free, dairy-free, soy-free, egg-free, fish-free, shellfish-free, nut-free

Nutrients per serving:

Carbohydrates – 41 g

Fat – 10 g

Protein – 3 g

Calories – 246

Ingredients:

- ¼ cup gluten-free flour blend
- ½ cup unsweetened cocoa powder
- 1 teaspoon baking soda
- ½ teaspoon baking powder
- ½ teaspoon of sea salt
- 1 cup of coconut sugar
- ⅓ cup coconut oil, melted
- 2 ripe bananas
- 1 teaspoon vanilla extract
- 1 teaspoon apple cider vinegar
- ⅜ cup of water

Instructions:

1. Preheat the oven to 350°F.
2. Line a loaf pan with parchment paper.
3. Whisk together all the dry ingredients.
4. Mash the bananas in another bowl.
5. Add the vanilla extract, apple cider vinegar, melted coconut oil, and water. Stir well.
6. Combine the wet and dry ingredients.
7. Pour the batter into the prepared pan.
8. Bake for 40-45 minutes.

Fruity Smoothie

Prep time: 10 minutes

Cooking time: 0 minutes

Servings: 1

Suitable for: gluten-free, dairy-free, soy-free, egg-free, fish-free, shellfish-free, nut-free, spices-free

Nutrients per serving:

Carbohydrates – 67 g

Fat – 7 g

Protein – 6 g

Calories – 333

Ingredients:

- ¾ cup frozen raspberries
- ¾ cup frozen mango
- ½ cup frozen pineapple
- ¾ cup calcium-fortified orange juice
- ½ Tbsp chia seeds

Instructions:

1. Place all the frozen fruits in the blender and let them defrost for a few minutes.
2. Add the chia seeds and juice and blend on high speed until smooth.

Avocado Smoothie

Prep time: 5 minutes

Cooking time: 0 minutes

Servings: 8

Suitable for: gluten-free, dairy-free, soy-free, egg-free, fish-free, shellfish-free, nut-free

Nutrients per serving:

Carbohydrates – 17 g

Fat – 39 g

Protein – 5 g

Calories – 409

Ingredients:

- ½ cup full-fat coconut milk
- ½ cup of coconut water
- ½ avocado
- ¼ cup baby spinach
- 1 handful of fresh parsley
- 1 drop stevia extract

Instructions:

1. Blend all the ingredients in a food processor until smooth.
2. Enjoy!

MAIN COURSES & SIDE DISHES

Cornbread

Prep time: 15 minutes

Cooking time: 2 hours

Servings: 8

Suitable for: gluten-free, dairy-free, soy-free, egg-free, fish-free, shellfish-free, nut-free

Nutrients per serving:

Carbohydrates – 41 g

Fat – 14 g

Protein – 5 g

Calories – 311

Ingredients:

For the cornbread:

- 6 Tablespoons vegan buttery spread melted
- 1½ cups yellow cornmeal
- 1 cup gluten-free flour blend
- 3½ teaspoons baking powder
- 5 Tablespoons unsweetened applesauce
- 2 Tablespoons sugar
- 1¼ teaspoons salt
- 1⅛ cup of any non-dairy milk

For the stuffing:

- ¼ cup vegan buttery spread
- 1 large sweet onion chopped
- 4 stalks celery chopped
- ½ cup fresh parsley chopped
- 1 teaspoon Italian seasoning
- 1 teaspoon salt
- ¼ teaspoon pepper
- 2½ cups vegetable broth

Instructions:

1. Preheat the oven to 350°F.
2. Whisk together the cornmeal, baking powder, sugar, salt, and gluten-free flour.
3. Add the applesauce, non-dairy milk, and vegan buttery spread. Combine.
4. Pour into the lightly grease a 9x13 inch pan. Bake for 20-24 minutes.
5. When the cornbread is cool, slice it. Place it on a baking sheet to dry for a day.
6. For the stuffing, preheat the oven to 375°F.
7. Melt the vegan buttery spread in a skillet over medium-low heat.
8. Add the chopped onions and celery and simmer for about 8-10 minutes.
9. Add the broth and, Italian seasoning, pepper, salt, and half of the chopped parsley. Bring to a boil then reduce heat to low.
10. Place the dried cornbread cubes in a 9x13 pan.
11. Pour the broth over the cornbread. Top with the remaining parsley and Bake for 20-30 minutes.

Guacamole

Prep time: 10 minutes

Cooking time: 10 minutes

Servings: 6

Suitable for: gluten-free, dairy-free, soy-free, egg-free, fish-free, shellfish-free, nut-free

Nutrients per serving:

Carbohydrates – 9 g

Fat – 14 g

Protein – 2 g

Calories – 162

Ingredients:

- 3 avocados, peeled and pits removed
- 1 garlic clove crushed
- 2 Tablespoons lemon juice
- ½ cup cilantro leaves
- 2 Tablespoons finely chopped red onion
- Sea salt to taste
- Pepper to taste

Instruction:

1. Combine all the ingredients in a bowl, using a potato masher to mix together.
2. Add the sea salt and black pepper to taste.
3. Serve immediately with tortilla chips.

Cheesy Cauliflower

Prep time: 10 minutes

Cooking time: 30 minutes

Servings: 4

Suitable for: gluten-free, dairy-free, soy-free, egg-free, fish-free, shellfish-free, nut-free

Nutrients per serving:

Carbohydrates – 3 g

Fat – 13 g

Protein – 2 g

Calories – 139

Ingredients:

- 1 head cauliflower
- ¼ cup olive oil
- ¼ cup nutritional yeast
- 1 teaspoon garlic powder
- ⅓ teaspoon salt
- ¼ teaspoon black pepper

Instructions:

1. Heat the oven to 425°F.
2. Place the cauliflower florets in a bowl.
3. Add the olive oil, garlic powder, salt, pepper, and nutritional yeast. Toss to coat.
4. Bake for 30 minutes.

Carrot-Cauliflower Soup

Prep time: 15 minutes

Cooking time: 30 minutes

Servings: 6

Suitable for: gluten-free, dairy-free, soy-free, egg-free, fish-free, shellfish-free, nut-free

Nutrients per serving:

Carbohydrates – 13 g

Fat – 3 g

Protein – 2 g

Calories – 85

Ingredients:

- 3 Tablespoons olive oil
- 1 onion chopped
- 2 cups chopped carrots
- 1 head chopped cauliflower florets
- 4 cups vegetable or chicken broth
- 2 teaspoons curry powder
- 1 teaspoon garlic powder
- 1 teaspoon salt
- ¼ teaspoon pepper
- ¼ non-dairy coconut milk

Instructions:

1. Fry chopped onions in olive oil in a large soup pot, over medium heat until soft, about 5 minutes.
2. Add chopped carrots and fry for a few minutes. Add the cauliflower, broth, curry powder, and garlic powder and raise the heat to high.
3. Bring to a boil then reduce the heat to simmer.
4. Cook until vegetables are tender.
5. Remove the pot from the heat and puree the soup using an immersion blender.
6. Add the non-dairy milk, salt, and pepper, and stir.
7. Top with fresh herbs, chopped red pepper, or sliced green onions

Dark Hummus

Prep time: 5 minutes

Cooking time: 0 minutes

Servings: 5

Suitable for: gluten-free, dairy-free, soy-free, egg-free, fish-free, shellfish-free, nut-free

Nutrients per serving:

Carbohydrates – 28 g

Fat – 7 g

Protein – 11 g

Calories – 221

Ingredients:

- 2 cloves fresh garlic minced
- ½ cup fresh cilantro
- 15 ounces canned black drained beans
- 2 Tblsp sunbutter
- 1 Tblsp canola oil
- 2 Tblsp fresh lemon juice
- ½ tsp salt

Instructions:

1. Place all ingredients in a food processor and process until smooth.
2. Place the hummus in a bowl and garnish with more cilantro if desired.
3. Serve with chips or crackers.

Stuffed Mushrooms

Prep time: 10 minutes

Cooking time: 30 minutes

Servings: 6

Suitable for: gluten-free, dairy-free, soy-free,
egg-free, fish-free, shellfish-free,
nut-free

Nutrients per serving:

Carbohydrates – 14 g

Fat – 5 g

Protein – 5 g

Calories – 117

Ingredients:

- 3 Yukon Gold potatoes, peel and cut into pieces
- 20 white button mushrooms
- 3 Tablespoons vegan buttery spread
- 3 Tablespoons unsweetened coconut milk
- ½ cup frozen chopped spinach
- ¼ Tablespoons curry powder
- 1 teaspoon Garam Masala
- ¼ teaspoon turmeric
- 1 teaspoon of sea salt
- ⅓ teaspoon pepper

Instructions:

1. Preheat the oven to 350°F.
2. Place clean mushrooms on a baking sheet and bake for about 30 minutes.
3. In the meantime, boil the potatoes for 15 minutes.
4. Drain the potatoes, then add coconut milk, vegan buttery spread, and spices.
5. To make the mixture smooth, use a potato masher. Add the spinach and stir until heated through.
6. Take out the mushrooms from the oven.
7. Set the oven to 450°F.
8. Fill each mushroom with the potato mixture.
9. Put the filled mushrooms in the oven for about 5 minutes.

Broccoli Salad

Prep time: 15 minutes

Cooking time: 0 minutes

Servings: 10

Suitable for: gluten-free, dairy-free, soy-free, egg-free, fish-free, shellfish-free, nut-free, , spices-free

Nutrients per serving:

Carbohydrates – 24 g

Fat – 27 g

Protein – 9 g

Calories – 369

Ingredients:

- 3 broccoli crowns, chopped into small pieces
- ½ cup red onion chopped fine
- Buttery vegan slices bacon cooked and crumbled
- ⅔ cup craisins
- ½ cup sunflower seeds optional
- For the dressing:
- 1 cup vegan mayonnaise
- 3 Tblsp organic cane sugar
- 2 Tblsp apple vinegar

Instructions:

1. Put the chopped broccoli, red onion, bacon, craisins, sunflower seeds into a bowl.
2. To make the salad dressing, stir together all dressing ingredients.
3. Add the dressing to the salad and mix.
4. Enjoy!

Carrot Fingers

Prep time: 15 minutes

Cooking time: 20 minutes

Servings: 5

Suitable for: gluten-free, dairy-free, soy-free,
egg-free, fish-free, shellfish-free,
nut-free, spices-free

Nutrients per serving:

Carbohydrates – 18 g

Fat – 6 g

Protein – 0 g

Calories – 130

Ingredients:

- 16 ounces frozen carrots
- 3½ Tbsp vegan buttery spread or regular butter
- 4 Tbsp brown sugar or coconut sugar
- ½ teaspoon sea salt

Instructions:

1. Melt the buttery spread in a saucepan over medium heat.
2. Add the carrots and cook until hot.
3. Add the sugar and salt.
4. Stir until carrots are well coated.

Quinoa Bowls

Prep time: 10 minutes

Cooking time: 20 minutes

Servings: 2

Suitable for: gluten-free, dairy-free, soy-free, egg-free, fish-free, shellfish-free, nut-free

Nutrients per serving:

Carbohydrates – 69 g

Fat – 26 g

Protein – 16 g

Calories – 551

Ingredients:

- ⅔ cup quinoa
- 1 red onion
- 1 Tbsp of olive oil
- 2 zucchini small zucchini sliced
- 1 cup frozen corn kernels thawed
- ¼ cup nutritional yeast
- ½ teaspoon mustard powder
- ½ teaspoon cumin
- 2 teaspoons garlic powder
- ½ teaspoon salt
- ¼ teaspoon pepper
- red pepper flakes
- 1 avocado

Instructions:

1. Cook the quinoa.
2. Fry the onion with zucchini in the olive oil.
3. Add the corn and cook until heated through. Season with salt and pepper.
4. Add the cumin, garlic powder, nutritional yeast, salt, and pepper.
5. Put the quinoa into bowls.
6. Top with avocado.

Spinach Quesadillas

Prep time: 5 minutes

Cooking time: 5 minutes

Servings: 2

Suitable for: gluten-free, dairy-free, soy-free, egg-free, fish-free, shellfish-free, nut-free

Nutrients per serving:

Carbohydrates – 51 g

Fat – 20 g

Protein – 11 g

Calories – 432

Ingredients:

- 1 Tablespoon vegan buttery spread
- 1 gluten-free tortilla
- 3 slices deli turkey
- ¼ cup sweet potato, mashed
- ⅓ cup fresh spinach
- ¼ cup vegan cheese

Instructions:

1. Put the vegan buttery spread in a frying pan and let melt over medium heat.
2. Add a gluten-free tortilla to the pan.
3. On the one side of the tortilla, spread the mashed sweet potatoes, then add the turkey, cheese, and spinach.
4. Fold the tortilla over.
5. Cook for a few minutes to brown, then carefully flip and cook for a few more minutes until the cheese is melted and the tortilla is golden brown.
6. Slice in half and serve!

Fruit Salad

Prep time: 10 minutes

Cooking time: 0 minutes

Servings: 4

Suitable for: gluten-free, dairy-free, soy-free, egg-free, fish-free, shellfish-free, nut-free, spices-free

Nutrients per serving:

Carbohydrates – 28 g

Fat – 2 g

Protein – 1 g

Calories – 125

Ingredients:

- 2 apples, sliced
- Mixed greens or spring mix
- 1 cup mandarin oranges in juice, drained
- ¼ cup pomegranate seeds
- 2 Tablespoons unsweetened coconut flakes

Instructions:

1. Combine all ingredients in a large bowl.
2. Divide among bowls and serve.

Lentil Burger

Prep time: 5 minutes

Cooking time: 35 minutes

Servings: 6

Suitable for: gluten-free, dairy-free, soy-free,
egg-free, fish-free, shellfish-free,
nut-free

Nutrients per serving:

Carbohydrates – 52 g

Fat – 4 g

Protein – 15 g

Calories – 311

Ingredients:

- 1 Tablespoon olive oil
- 1¼ cup green lentils, harvested and washed
- 1 chopped onion
- 8 ounces tomato sauce
- 2 tablespoons mustard
- 1 teaspoon apple vinegar
- 1 Tablespoon granulated sugar
- 1 teaspoon of sea salt
- ½ teaspoon pepper
- 2 teaspoons cumin
- ½ teaspoon chili powder
- 1 teaspoon garlic powder
- 1 teaspoon paprika
- 6 hamburger gluten-free buns
- ½ cup chopped onion for topping

Instructions:

1. Place the lentils in a pot with enough water to cover them.
2. Bring to a boil. Cover with a lid tilted to vent out the steam.
3. Cook about 25-30 minutes.
4. Put the onion into a pan with the olive oil and cook on medium heat for about 6-7 minutes.
5. Add the lentils to the onions, and stir.
6. Add the remaining ingredients, and cook over medium-low heat for about 15 minutes.

Cheesy-Spinach Rice

Prep time: 5 minutes

Cooking time: 40 minutes

Servings: 4

Suitable for: gluten-free, dairy-free, soy-free,
egg-free, fish-free, shellfish-free,
nut-free, vegetables/fruits free

Nutrients per serving:

Carbohydrates – 49 g

Fat – 8 g

Protein – 6 g

Calories – 303

Ingredients:

- 1 cup organic short grain brown rice
- 1 teaspoon olive oil
- 1 small onion chopped
- 3 cloves garlic thinly sliced
- 1 cup dairy-free mozzarella cheese
- 1 cup frozen chopped spinach, thawed and dried
- ⅔ cup dairy-free milk of your choice
- 1 tablespoon gluten-free flour mixture
- 1 teaspoon of sea salt
- ¼ teaspoon of pepper
- ½ teaspoon garlic powder
- water

Instructions:

1. In a pot, combine the olive oil, brown rice, chopped onion, garlic, and ¾ cups of water. Bring to a boil and cook about 35-40 minutes.
2. When rice is done cooking, add the spinach and dairy-free cheese. Stir until cheese is melted.
3. Add the dairy-free milk and gluten-free blend flour. Stir well.
4. Add the sea salt, pepper, and garlic powder.

Frittata

Prep time: 5 minutes

Cooking time: 20 minutes

Servings: 6

Suitable for: gluten-free, dairy-free, soy-free, fish-free, shellfish-free, nut-free

Nutrients per serving:

Carbohydrates – 5 g

Fat – 7 g

Protein – 10 g

Calories –136

Ingredients:

- 8 eggs (if you are allergic to eggs, you can use just the yolk)
- 1 Yukon gold potato, peeled and diced
- ¼ cup onion, chopped
- ½ cup ham, diced
- ¾ cup baby spinach
- ¼ cup water or non-dairy milk

Instructions:

1. Preheat oven to 400°F.
2. Whisk together the eggs, and water, pepper, and salt.
3. Add remaining ingredients and mix.
4. Bake for 20 minutes in a deep dish pie plate.
5. Enjoy!

Salsa

Prep time: 10 minutes

Cooking time: 20 minutes

Servings: 6

Suitable for: gluten-free, dairy-free, soy-free, egg-free, fish-free, shellfish-free, nut-free

Nutrients per serving:

Carbohydrates – 5 g

Fat – 0 g

Protein – 1 g

Calories – 6

Ingredients:

- ½ small sweet onion
- 3 cloves garlic
- 3 cups cherry tomatoes
- ½ cup cilantro leaves, packed
- 1 lime juiced
- Salt, to taste

Instructions:

1. Process the garlic with onion in a food processor until paste.
2. Add cherry tomatoes and cilantro and pulse until the tomatoes are finely chopped.
3. If there is a lot of excess fluid, drain it.
4. Stir in lime juice and salt.
5. Serve with tortilla chips.

DESSERTS & SNACKS

Chocolate Cubes

Prep time: 5 minutes

Cooking time: 5 minutes

Servings: 36

Suitable for: gluten-free, dairy-free, soy-free, egg-free, fish-free, shellfish-free, nut-free, vegetables/fruits free, spices-free.

Nutrients per serving:

Calories – 106

Protein – 1 g

Fat – 7 g

Carbohydrates – 11 g

Sugar – 9 g

Ingredients:

- 13.5 ounces of canned coconut milk
- ¾ cup confectioner's sugar
- 3 cups dairy-free dark chocolate chips

Instructions:

1. Line a square pan with parchment paper, leaving some overhang.
2. In a pan over medium-low heat, add the coconut milk.
3. Add the confectioner's sugar and whisk. Do not let it boil.
4. Add the chocolate chips and stir until fully melted.
5. Pour mixture into the square pan and spread out with a spatula.
6. Cool for 30 minutes, then refrigerate for 2 hours.
7. Using the overhang of parchment paper, remove your treat from the pan, then slice into squares.
8. Enjoy!

Apple Crisps

Prep time: 15 minutes

Cooking time: 45 minutes

Servings: 9

Suitable for: gluten-free, dairy-free, soy-free,
egg-free, fish-free, shellfish-free,
nut-free

Nutrients per serving:

Carbohydrates – 56 g

Fat – 18 g

Protein – 5 g

Calories – 411

Ingredients:

- 1 cup gluten-free oat flour
- ⅔ cup pumpkin seeds
- ½ cup gluten-free oats
- ⅓ cup organic cane sugar
- ½ cup vegan buttery spread
- pinch sea salt
- 2 tbsp water

For the apple filling:

- 3 apples peeled and sliced thin
- 3 tbsp organic cane sugar
- 1 tsp cinnamon
- ½ tsp ground ginger

For the topping:

- 1 tbsp vegan buttery spread
- 1 cup gluten-free oats
- ¼ cup gluten-free oats flour
- ⅔ cup light brown sugar
- ¾ tsp cinnamon
- ¼ tsp salt

Instructions:

1. Preheat the oven to 350°F.
2. Pulse the pumpkin seeds in a food

processor.
3. Combine ground pumpkin seeds, the oat flour, oats, sea salt, organic cane sugar, and the vegan buttery spread.
4. Add the 2 Tbsp of water and mix.
5. Place the dough in an eight-inch square glass baking pan and use your hands to spread it out and pat it down. Bake for 10 minutes.
6. For the apple filling, combine the sliced apples, cinnamon, ground ginger, and sugar in a bowl. Stir it well.
7. To make the topping, mix the oats, oat flour, brown sugar, cinnamon, salt, and vegan buttery spread together. Use a pastry cutter until the oat mixture resembles a crumbly topping.
8. Spread the apples evenly over the crust.
9. Sprinkle the buttery oat topping all over the apples.
10. Bake for 35-40 minutes.
11. Let cool for 20 minutes.
12. Enjoy!

Unusual Chocolate Mousse

Prep time: 5 minutes

Cooking time: 0 minutes

Servings: 2

Suitable for: gluten-free, dairy-free, soy-free, egg-free, fish-free, shellfish-free, nut-free

Nutrients per serving:

Carbohydrates – 38 g

Fat – 18 g

Protein – 5 g

Calories – 311

Ingredients:

- 1 large avocado, sliced
- 8 sweet cherries, pitted and stems removed
- 3 Tbsp unsweetened cocoa powder
- 2-3 Tbsp maple syrup
- 6 Tbsp of any non-dairy milk
- ½ tsp vanilla extract
- 1 Tbsp dairy-free chocolate chips

Instructions:

1. Process avocado, cherries, cocoa, maple syrup, milk and vanilla extract in a food processor until creamy.
2. Add more maple syrup or cocoa powder if needed. This will depend on the avocado size.
3. Top with chocolate chips and serve.

Spicy Pumpkin Cookies

Prep time: 10 minutes

Cooking time: 12 minutes

Servings: 24 cookies

Suitable for: gluten-free, dairy-free, soy-free, egg-free, fish-free, shellfish-free, nut-free

Nutrients per serving:

Carbohydrates – 15 g

Fat – 3 g

Protein – 1 g

Calories – 92

Ingredients:

- 2 cups gluten-free flour blend
- ½ cup vegan buttery spread
- ½ cup organic cane sugar
- ¼ cup light brown sugar
- ⅛ cup molasses
- 1 teaspoon vanilla extract
- ⅓ cup pure pumpkin puree
- ¾ teaspoons cinnamon
- ½ teaspoon ginger
- ¼ teaspoon nutmeg
- pinch of cloves
- ⅛ teaspoon salt
- 1 teaspoon baking soda
- sugar for rolling

Instructions:

1. Preheat oven to 350°F.
2. Line a cookie sheet with parchment paper.
3. Whisk together the gluten-free flour,

   ginger, nutmeg, cinnamon, cloves, baking soda, and salt.
4. Cream the vegan buttery spread and sugars, then add the molasses, pumpkin puree, and vanilla extract and mix until smooth.
5. Combine all the wet ingredients and all the dry ingredients.
6. Pour a few tablespoons of sugar for rolling in a small bowl.
7. Make medium-sized balls out of the dough and roll them in sugar and press to make a cookie shape.
8. Bake for 10-12 minutes.

Muddy-Buddies Snack

Prep time: 5 minutes

Cooking time: 2 minutes

Servings: 12

Suitable for: gluten-free, dairy-free, soy-free, egg-free, fish-free, shellfish-free, nut-free, vegetables/fruits free, spices-free

Nutrients per serving:

Carbohydrates – 50 g

Fat – 10 g

Protein – 4 g

Calories – 301

Ingredients:

- 9 cups of corn cereal
- ¼ cups dairy-free chocolate chips
- ½ cup sunbutter
- ½ cups powdered sugar

Instructions:

1. Microwave the chocolate chips for 60 seconds. Stir, then microwave for 15 seconds intervals until melted.
2. Stir in the sunbutter until smooth.
3. Add the cereal to the bowl and stir until the cereal is covered.
4. Pour the mixture into two Ziploc bags. Add half of the powdered sugar into each bag, then seal the bags and shake well.
5. Pour into a serving bowl and enjoy!

Almond-Banana Muffins

Prep time: 5 minutes

Cooking time: 18 minutes

Servings: 12

Suitable for: gluten-free, dairy-free, soy-free, egg-free, fish-free, shellfish-free, spices-free

Nutrients per serving:

Carbohydrates – 10 g

Fat – 8 g

Protein – 2 g

Calories – 116

Ingredients

- ⅛ cup coconut oil, melted
- ¼ cup sugar
- 1 cup almond meal
- 1 ripe banana
- ¼ cup dairy-free chocolate chips

Instructions:

1. Preheat the oven to 350°F.
2. Line a muffin tin with paper liners.
3. In a medium bowl, mash the overripe banana with a fork.
4. Add the coconut oil, sugar, and almond meal. Mix together.
5. Add the mini chocolate chips. Stir.
6. Spoon into prepared muffin tin.
7. Bake for 18-20 minutes.
8. Cool on a wire rack.

Cherry-Chia-Peach Pudding

Prep time: 14 minutes

Cooking time: 4 hours

Servings: 2

Suitable for: gluten-free, dairy-free, soy-free,
egg-free, fish-free, shellfish-free,
nut-free

Nutrients per serving:

Carbohydrates – 61 g

Fat – 12 g

Protein – 10 g

Calories – 391

Ingredients:

- 1 cup of any non-dairy milk
- 5½ Tbsp chia seeds
- 3 Tbsp maple syrup
- 1½ tsp vanilla extract
- 2 peaches, diced
- ¾ cup cherries, pitted and sliced
- 1 tsp honey

Instructions:

1. Combine the chia seeds, non-dairy milk, maple syrup, and vanilla extract in a container with a lid. Stir well.
2. Refrigerate for 4 hours.
3. Stir mixture before serving, and top with diced peaches and cherries. Drizzle honey over top.

Chocolate Energy Balls

Prep time: 10 minutes

Cooking time: 10 minutes

Servings: 24

Suitable for: gluten-free, dairy-free, soy-free, egg-free, fish-free, shellfish-free, nut-free, vegetables/fruits free

Nutrients per serving:

Carbohydrates – 16 g

Fat – 5 g

Protein – 5 g

Calories – 133

Ingredients:

- 1 cup pumpkin seeds
- 1 cup hemp hearts
- 1 cup dried cherries
- 1 cup unsweetened cocoa powder
- 1 cup maple syrup
- ¼ cup dairy-free chocolate chips
- Extra cocoa powder for rolling

Instructions:

1. Put hemp hearts and the pumpkin seeds in a food processor and pulse until finely ground.
2. Add the dried cherries, cocoa powder, and maple syrup. Process until the mixture is fairly smooth, though it will be quite thick.
3. Add the chocolate chips and stir.
4. Line a cookie sheet with waxed paper.
5. Roll mixture into balls, then dip in cocoa powder. Place the balls on the cookie sheet.
6. Refrigerate for about an hour.
7. Enjoy!

Cinnamon Cookies

Prep time: 10 minutes

Cooking time: 16 minutes

Servings: 4

Suitable for: gluten-free, dairy-free, soy-free, egg-free, fish-free, shellfish-free, nut-free, vegetables/fruits free

Nutrients per serving:

Carbohydrates – 28 g

Fat – 4 g

Protein – 3 g

Calories – 163

Ingredients:

- ½ cup gluten-free oats
- ⅝ cup gluten-free flour blend
- ⅛ teaspoon salt
- 1½ Tablespoons organic cane sugar
- 1 teaspoon cinnamon
- 1½ Tablespoons vegan buttery spread melted
- 1 Tablespoon maple syrup
- ⅛ cup water
- Cinnamon to taste
- Sugar to taste

Instructions:

1. Preheat the oven to 400°F.
2. Process gluten-free oats in the food processor until creamy.
3. Stir in the melted vegan buttery spread, maple syrup, and sugar.
4. Add the oat flour, gluten-free flour blend, cinnamon, and salt.
5. Add a little bit of water, alternating with stirring.
6. Place the ball of dough on parchment paper, and lay another piece of parchment paper on top.
7. Roll the dough into ⅛ inch.
8. Cut the dough into circles. Dust with cinnamon sugar.
9. Bake for 13-16 minutes.

Pumpkin Dessert

Prep time: 10 minutes

Cooking time: 10 minutes

Servings: 6

Suitable for: gluten-free, dairy-free, soy-free, egg-free, fish-free, shellfish-free, nut-free, vegetables/fruits free

Nutrients per serving:

Carbohydrates – 39 g

Fat – 9 g

Protein – 3 g

Calories – 250

Ingredients:

- 9 ounces Cocoa Whip thawed
- 5/8 cup pure pumpkin puree
- 3/4 cup powdered sugar
- 3/4 teaspoon cinnamon
- 1/4 teaspoon ground ginger
- 12 gluten-free cookies of your choice
- 1½ Tablespoons vegan buttery spread
- 2 Tablespoons pumpkin seeds

Instructions:

1. Process the cookies and the vegan buttery spread on high speed to form crumbs. Set aside.
2. In another bowl, mix together the cocoa whip, pumpkin puree, powdered sugar, cinnamon, and ginger. Refrigerate for 1 hour.
3. Place some crumbs in small bowls. Spoon in some of the chilled pumpkin mousses. Top with pumpkin seeds and more crumbs.
4. Enjoy!

Chocolate Bars

Prep time: 10 minutes

Cooking time: 5 minutes

Servings: 10

Suitable for: gluten-free, dairy-free, soy-free, egg-free, fish-free, shellfish-free, nut-free

Nutrients per serving:

Carbohydrates – 13 g

Fat – 6 g

Protein – 2 g

Calories – 107

Ingredients:

- 1 cup Medjool dates pitted
- 1 cup pumpkin seeds
- ½ cup unsweetened coconut flakes
- 2 Tablespoons unsweetened cocoa powder
- ½ teaspoon vanilla extract

Instructions:

1. Preheat the oven to 325°F.
2. Put the coconut flakes on a cookie sheet and bake for 6 minutes. Let cool.
3. Process the pitted dates, pumpkin seeds, toasted coconut, unsweetened cocoa powder, and vanilla extract in a food processor until all the ingredients come together into a ball.
4. Spread the mixture on a piece of parchment paper
5. Refrigerate for two hours.
6. Slice into 10 bars.

Blackberry Cupcake

Prep time: 2 minutes

Cooking time: 1 minute

Servings: 1

Suitable for: gluten-free, dairy-free, soy-free, egg-free, fish-free, shellfish-free, nut-free, spices-free

Nutrients per serving:

Carbohydrates – 62 g

Fat – 22 g

Protein – 6 g

Calories – 420

Ingredients:

- 2 Tablespoons gluten-free flour blend
- ½ Tablespoons coconut sugar
- ¾ Tablespoon unsweetened cocoa powder
- 1 teaspoon organic canola oil
- ⅛ teaspoon baking soda
- Pinch of salt
- ⅛ teaspoon vinegar
- 2½ - 3 Tablespoons water
- ½ Tablespoons dairy-free dark chocolate chips
- 10-12 fresh blackberries

Instructions:

1. Whisk together the gluten-free flour, unsweetened cocoa powder, coconut sugar, baking soda, and salt.
2. Add the vinegar, canola oil, water, and stir.
3. Add the fresh blackberries and dark chocolate chips. Stir well.
4. Microwave at 70% power for 70 seconds.
5. Enjoy! You can top this with dairy-free yogurt, ice cream, more fresh fruit, or anything you like.

Yellow Muffins

Prep time: 5 minutes

Cooking time: 18 minutes

Servings: 12

Suitable for: gluten-free, dairy-free, soy-free, egg-free, fish-free, shellfish-free, nut-free, vegetables/fruits free, spices-free

Nutrients per serving:

Carbohydrates – 26 g

Fat – 6 g

Protein – 3 g

Calories – 182

Ingredients:

- 1½ cups yellow cornmeal
- 1 cup white spelled flour or a gluten-free flour blend
- 3 Tablespoons organic cane sugar
- 3½ teaspoons baking powder
- 1¼ teaspoons sea salt
- 5 Tablespoons unsweetened applesauce
- 6 Tablespoons vegan buttery spread melted
- 1 ⅛ cup any non-dairy milk
- ½ cup corn kernels

Instructions:

1. Preheat the oven to 350°F.
2. Whisk together the cornmeal, flour, organic sea salt, cane sugar, and baking powder.
3. Add the non-dairy milk, applesauce, and melted vegan buttery spread.
4. Add the corn kernels.
5. Let the batter stay for a few minutes – it should puff up.
6. Gently spoon the batter into the paper muffin tin.
7. Bake for 16-19 minutes.

Bars with Marshmallows

Prep time: 10 minutes

Cooking time: 25 minutes

Servings: 9

Suitable for: gluten-free, dairy-free, soy-free, egg-free, fish-free, shellfish-free, nut-free, vegetables/fruits free, spices-free

Nutrients per serving:

Carbohydrates – 36 g

Fat – 14 g

Protein – 2 g

Calories – 271

Ingredients:

- 1 cup gluten-free graham cracker crumbs
- ¾ cup dairy free chocolate chips
- ¾ cup gluten-free flour blend
- ⅜ cup sugar
- ½ cup vegan buttery spread
- 1 cup mini marshmallows

Instructions:

1. Preheat the oven to 350°F.
2. Combine the cracker crumbs, gluten-free flour blend, buttery spread, and sugar in a food processor and pulse until a dough forms.
3. Put into the 8x8 baking pan and line with parchment paper, and bake for 15-18 minutes.
4. Remove the pan from the oven, and raise the heat to 375°F.
5. Sprinkle the chocolate chips, then the marshmallows on the baked dough.
6. Bake for 5-7 minutes.

Banana's Snack

Prep time: 5 minutes

Cooking time: 10 minutes

Servings: 24

Suitable for: gluten-free, dairy-free, soy-free, egg-free, fish-free, shellfish-free, nut-free

Nutrients per serving:

Carbohydrates – 12 g

Fat – 5 g

Protein – 2 g

Calories – 104

Ingredients:

- 1 banana, pureed
- 1 cup peanut butter
- 1 cup dark brown sugar
- ½ tsp vanilla extract
- 1 teaspoon baking soda
- 1 tablespoon ground flax

Instructions:

1. Preheat oven to 350°F.
2. Mix all the ingredients.
3. Spoon dough onto baking sheet.
4. Bake for 8-10 minutes.

Cranberry Cookies

Prep time: 10 minutes

Cooking time: 11 minutes

Servings: 24

Suitable for: gluten-free, dairy-free, soy-free, egg-free, fish-free, shellfish-free, nut-free

Nutrients per serving:

Carbohydrates – 17 g

Fat – 5 g

Protein – 1 g

Calories –118

Ingredients:

- ½ cup vegan buttery spread
- ½ cup light brown sugar
- ½ cup of organic cane sugar
- 1 Tablespoon flax seed meal
- 3 Tablespoons water
- 1 teaspoon vanilla extract
- 1 cup gluten-free flour blend
- ½ teaspoon baking soda
- ½ teaspoon of sea salt
- 1½ cups gluten free old fashioned oats
- ¾ cups fresh cranberries
- 1 cup dairy-free chocolate chips

Instructions:

1. Preheat the oven to 350°F.
2. Line a cookie sheet with parchment paper.
3. Add water to the ground flax seed and let soak for 4 minutes.
4. Combine the gluten-free blend flour, sea salt, and baking soda.
5. Whisk together the vegan buttery spread and sugars.
6. Add the vanilla extract and flax seed .
7. Add all the dry ingredients. Mix well.
8. Add the gluten free oats, chocolate chips, and cranberries. Stir well.
9. Drop dough by tablespoonfuls on the cookie sheet.
10. Bake for about 10 minutes.

Lace Cookies

Prep time: 10 minutes

Cooking time: 10 minutes

Servings: 40

Suitable for: gluten-free, dairy-free, soy-free, egg-free, fish-free, shellfish-free, nut-free, vegetables/fruits free

Nutrients per serving:

Carbohydrates – 10 g

Fat – 4 g

Protein – 0 g

Calories – 85

Ingredients:

- ½ cup vegan buttery spread
- 1 cup of organic cane sugar
- 1 teaspoon vanilla extract
- 2 Tablespoons unsweetened applesauce
- 1 cup gluten-free oats
- ¼ cup gluten-free flour
- ½ teaspoon salt
- ½ cup dairy-free milk chocolate chips

Instructions

1. Preheat oven to 325°F.
2. Line two baking sheets with parchment paper.
3. Combine the vegan cream spread, organic cane sugar, and vanilla extract in a bowl. Mix with a blender at medium speed until fluffy.
4. Stir in the unsweetened applesauce.

5. Add the gluten-free oats, gluten-free flour blend, and salt and stir until combined.
6. Drop teaspoons of the dough on the baking sheets.
7. Bake for about 8-10 minutes.
8. Put the dairy-free chocolate chips in a microwave safe bowl and microwave for one minute.
9. Stir, then microwave in 15-second intervals until fully melted.
10. Decorate the cookies with the chocolate.
11. Refrigerate for a 3 minutes.

Chocolate Ice Cream

Prep time: 10 minutes

Cooking time: 6 hours

Servings: 8

Suitable for: gluten-free, dairy-free, soy-free, egg-free, fish-free, shellfish-free, nut-free, vegetables/fruits free

Nutrients per serving:

Carbohydrates – 19 g

Fat – 15 g

Protein – 3 g

Calories – 224

Ingredients:

- 11 ounces full fat coconut milk
- 2 Tablespoons sunbutter
- ¼ cup maple syrup
- 3 Tablespoons non-dairy milk
- 3 Tablespoons unsweetened cocoa powder
- 2 teaspoons vanilla extract
- 8 cups sunbutter

Instructions:

1. In a bowl, combine the coconut milk, maple syrup, and sunbutter.
2. Add the cocoa powder, vanilla extract, non-dairy milk.
3. Put some sunbutter at the bottom of each popsicle form.
4. Fill the forms halfway with the chocolate mixture.
5. Add more sunbutter, then more chocolate mixture.
6. Put a popsicle sticks in each.
7. Freeze for 8 hours.

Cheese Ball

Prep time: 10 minutes

Cooking time: 0 hours

Servings: 10

Suitable for: gluten-free, dairy-free, soy-free, egg-free, fish-free, shellfish-free, nut-free, vegetables/fruits free

Nutrients per serving:

Carbohydrates – 7 g

Fat – 15 g

Protein – 3 g

Calories – 173

Ingredients:

- 2 Tablespoons vegan buttery spread
- 7 ounces cubed any dairy-free cheese
- 8 ounces dairy-free plain cream cheese
- ¾ cup any seed of your choice
- ¼ teaspoon garlic powder
- ¼ teaspoon cumin

Instructions:

1. Pulse the seeds in a food processor.
2. Set aside two tablespoons of the seeds on a plate.
3. Add the diced cheese to the processor. Pulse until the cheese is finely chopped.
4. Add cream cheese, vegan butter spread, garlic powder, and cumin, and mix until smooth.
5. Take the cheese mixture and form into a ball.
6. Roll in the seeds until.
7. Wrap in plastic wrap and refrigerate for 1 hour before serving.

RECIPES FOR KIDS

Coconut Hot Chocolate

Prep time: 5 minutes

Cooking time: 10 minutes

Servings: 3

Suitable for: gluten-free, dairy-free, soy-free, egg-free, fish-free, shellfish-free, nut-free, vegetables/fruits free, spices-free

Nutrients per serving:

Carbohydrates – 12 g

Fat – 17 g

Protein – 3 g

Calories – 204

Ingredients:

- 8 ounces full fat unsweetened coconut milk
- 2 ounces dark chocolate
- 2 Tablespoons cane sugar
- ¾ cup of any non-dairy milk

Instructions:

1. Pour half of a can of full-fat unsweetened coconut milk into a small saucepan over medium-low heat.
2. Add the crushed dark chocolate, stir until the chocolate melted.
3. Add the cane sugar and stir well.
4. Stir in non-dairy milk .
5. Pour into cups or mugs. Serve with a marshmallow if desired.

Cherry Lollipops

Prep time: 15 minutes

Cooking time: 0 minutes

Servings: 30 cherries

Suitable for: gluten-free, dairy-free, soy-free, egg-free, fish-free, shellfish-free, nut-free, vegetables/fruits free, spices-free

Nutrients per serving:

Carbohydrates – 7 g

Fat – 2 g

Protein – 0 g

Calories – 50

Ingredients:

- 30 sweet cherries, pitted
- 1½ cups chocolate chips
- Sprinkles

Instructions:

1. Heat chocolate chips over medium-low heat, stirring well until melted.
2. Dip the cherries in the chocolate and set aside on the cookie sheet.
3. Decorate with sprinkles.
4. Refrigerate for at least one hour or until the chocolate is set.

Halloween Treats

Prep time: 10 minutes

Cooking time: 20 minutes

Servings: 5

Suitable for: gluten-free, dairy-free, soy-free, egg-free, fish-free, shellfish-free, nut-free, vegetables/fruits free, spices-free

Nutrients per serving:

Carbohydrates – 14 g

Fat – 10 g

Protein – 1 g

Calories – 156

Ingredients:

- ¾ cup dairy free chocolate chips

Instructions:

1. Microwave the chocolate chips for 45-60 seconds with 10-second intervals.
2. Place the melted chocolate into Halloween themed lollipop mold with sticks.
3. Refrigerate for about 20 minutes.

Pretzel Muffins

Prep time: 10 minutes

Cooking time: 1 hour

Servings: 6

Suitable for: gluten-free, dairy-free, soy-free, egg-free, fish-free, shellfish-free, nut-free, vegetables/fruits free, spices-free

Nutrients per serving:

Carbohydrates – 20 g

Fat – 6 g

Protein – 2 g

Calories – 149

Ingredients:

- 1 cup pretzels
- 2 Tablespoons vegan buttery spread
- 1 Tablespoon sugar
- 2 pinches salt
- 12 Tablespoons dairy-free chocolate ice cream softened
- 1 cup dairy-free chocolate chips

Instructions:

1. Crush pretzels into crumbs.
2. Melt buttery spread in the microwave and stir in the pretzel crumbs, salt, and sugar.
3. Put some of the crust mixture in each paper liner.
4. Add a tablespoon of chocolate ice cream in each cup.
5. Put whole pretzels or some chocolate chips on each ice cream bite.
6. Cover the muffin tin and freeze until firm, about 1 hour.

Dairy-Free Cocoa

Prep time: 5 minutes

Cooking time: 10 minutes

Servings: 3

Suitable for: gluten-free, dairy-free, soy-free, egg-free, fish-free, shellfish-free, nut-free, vegetables/fruits free

Nutrients per serving:

Carbohydrates – 43 g

Fat – 7 g

Protein – 12 g

Calories – 272

Ingredients:

- 3 cups non-dairy milk of your choice
- 5 Tablespoons cocoa powder
- 4 Tablespoons organic cane sugar
- ¼ teaspoon peppermint extract
- Allergy friendly candy canes and chocolate shavings

Instructions:

1. Heat non-dairy milk over medium heat until steaming, but do not let boil.
2. Add the cocoa powder and sugar and stir well.
3. Remove cocoa from the stove and add peppermint extract.
4. Pour the cocoa into mugs and top with chocolate shavings.
5. Add a candy cane and serve immediately.

Bunny Cookies

Prep time: 2 hours

Cooking time: 10 minutes

Servings: 24

Suitable for: gluten-free, dairy-free, soy-free,
egg-free, fish-free, shellfish-free,
nut-free, vegetables/fruits free

Nutrients per serving:

Carbohydrates – 28 g

Fat – 8 g

Protein – 1 g

Calories – 186

Ingredients:

- 1 cup vegan buttery spread
- 1 cup organic cane sugar
- ¼ cup unsweetened apple sauce
- 1 teaspoon vanilla extract
- 3 cups gluten-free flour blend
- ¼ teaspoon salt

Instructions:

1. Cream together the sugar and vegan buttery spread.
2. Mix in the vanilla extract and applesauce.
3. Add the salt and the gluten-free flour one cup at a time, mixing between each addition. The dough will be thick.
4. Divide your dough into two parts and make discs out of them. Wrap each disc with plastic wrap . Refrigerate for two hours.
5. Preheat the oven to 350°F .
6. Coat a rolling pin and surface with gluten-free flour.
7. Roll the dough until it is ¼ inch.
8. Cut out the shapes with a cookie cutter and place on a cookie sheet.
9. Bake for 10 minutes.

Healthy Apple Lollipops

Prep time: 10 minutes

Cooking time: 25 minutes

Servings: 10

Suitable for: gluten-free, dairy-free, soy-free, egg-free, fish-free, shellfish-free, nut-free, spices-free

Nutrients per serving:

Carbohydrates – 95 g

Fat – 21 g

Protein – 1 g

Calories – 551

Ingredients:

- 1 cup soy-free vegan buttery spread
- 2 cups light brown sugar, packed
- 1 cup light organic corn syrup
- 11 ounces full fat coconut milk
- ¼ teaspoon salt
- 10-12 tart apples
- Sprinles for decoration

Instructions:

1. Wash and dry apples.
2. Insert a popsicle stick into each apple.
3. Melt the vegan buttery spread over medium-high heat.
4. Add the brown sugar and stir until melted.
5. Add the coconut milk and corn syrup. Bring to a boil and cook, stirring constantly, for about 20 minutes.
6. Remove the pan from the heat and stir in the salt.
7. Dip the apples into the caramel, rotating to coat completely.
8. Place the dipped apples on a parchment lined cookie sheet.
9. Twist the apples once cool to remove from the parchment paper.
10. Decorate and serve!

Caramel Candies

Prep time: 5 minutes

Cooking time: 15 minutes

Servings: 32

Suitable for: gluten-free, dairy-free, soy-free, egg-free, fish-free, shellfish-free, nut-free, vegetables/fruits free, spices-free

Nutrients per serving:

Carbohydrates – 21 g

Fat – 6 g

Protein – 0 g

Calories – 142

Ingredients:

- 1 cup vegan buttery spread
- 2 cups brown sugar, packed
- ⅓ teaspoon sea salt
- 1 cup light organic corn syrup
- 11 ounces of coconut milk

Instructions:

1. Stick a candy thermometer in a pot so that the end is near the bottom, but not resting on it.
2. Melt the vegan buttery spread in the pot.
3. Add the brown sugar and stir until incorporated and melted.
4. Add the coconut milk and light organic corn syrup.

5. Bring this mixture to a boil and continue to cook, stirring constantly, until the candy thermometer reads 235°F.
6. Remove pan from heat and add sea salt.
7. Pour the caramel on a cookie sheet with a parchment paper. It should spread out, but you can use a rubber spatula to help smooth it out.
8. Let it cool, then slice. Wrap each caramel in squares of parchment paper.

Sweet Potato Fries

Prep time: 10 minutes

Cooking time: 20 minutes

Servings: 3

Suitable for: gluten-free, dairy-free, soy-free,
egg-free, fish-free, shellfish-free,
nut-free, spices-free

Nutrients per serving:

Carbohydrates – 20 g

Fat – 7 g

Protein – 1 g

Calories – 158

Ingredients:

- 2 Tablespoons olive oil
- 1 teaspoon garlic powder
- 1 teaspoon onion powder
- 2 large sweet potatoes peeled
- 2 tablespoons of olive oil
- Sea salt to taste

Instructions:

1. Preheat oven to 450°F.
2. Slice the sweet potatoes into thin strips.
3. Toss the sweet potato fries with the olive oil, garlic powder, and onion powder.
4. Spread out on two cookie sheets.
5. Bake for 20 minutes. Stir the fries every 5 minutes.

Blackberry Popsicle

Prep time: 5 minutes

Cooking time: 2 hours

Servings: 5

Suitable for: gluten-free, dairy-free, soy-free, egg-free, fish-free, shellfish-free, nut-free, spices-free

Nutrients per serving:

Carbohydrates – 10 g

Fat – 0 g

Protein – 1 g

Calories – 52

Ingredients:

- 6 ounces vanilla cultured coconut milk yogurt
- ½ cups blackberries
- ¼ Tablespoons sugar

Instructions:

1. Put the sugar and blackberries in the blender. Blend on high speed.
2. Place a fine strainer in a bowl. Pour blackberry puree into it and push through with a spoon.
3. Put the blackberry puree and the yogurt in popsicle molds.
4. Insert the sticks and freeze for 4 hours until firm.

Chessboard Cookies

Prep time: 4 hours

Cooking time: 10 minutes

Servings: 28

Suitable for: gluten-free, dairy-free, soy-free, egg-free, fish-free, shellfish-free, nut-free, vegetables/fruits free, spices-free

Nutrients per serving:

Carbohydrates – 17 g

Fat – 5 g

Protein – 1 g

Calories – 122

Ingredients:

For the vanilla dough:

- ½ cup vegan buttery spread
- ⅝ cup granulated sugar
- ⅛ cup unsweetened apple sauce
- 1½ cups gluten-free flour blend
- ⅛ teaspoon salt

For the chocolate dough:

- ½ cup vegan buttery spread
- ½ cup granulated sugar
- ⅛ cup brown sugar
- ⅛ cup unsweetened apple sauce
- 1 cup gluten-free flour blend
- ½ cup unsweetened cocoa powder
- ⅛ teaspoon of salt

Instructions:

1. Cream the buttery spread and the sugar.
2. Add the applesauce and vanilla.

3. Add the salt and gluten-free flour blend and mix until combined.
4. Cream the buttery spread and the sugar.
5. Add the applesauce and cocoa.
6. Add the gluten-free flour blend and salt and mix until combined.
7. Put the dough on plastic wrap and shape into a log, about two inches square. Wrap both doughs and put in the fridge for two hours.
8. When the dough is thoroughly chilled, remove from the refrigerator and press down on a hard surface. Do it with each side so that you get the edges nice and square.
9. Unwrap, and with a very sharp knife, cut each log into three even slices. Then cut each slice into three pieces.
10. Take the dough pieces and organize them into a checkerboard pattern.
11. Bake for 10 minutes.

French Toast

Prep time: 5 minutes

Cooking time: 12 minutes

Servings: 5

Suitable for: gluten-free, dairy-free, egg-free, fish-free, shellfish-free, nut-free

Nutrients per serving:

Carbohydrates – 14 g

Fat – 5 g

Protein – 3 g

Calories – 165

Ingredients:

- ¾ cup non-dairy milk
- 2 Tablespoons vegan buttery spread
- 1 Tablespoon potato starch
- ¼ teaspoon cinnamon
- Pinch salt
- 5 slices gluten-free bread

Instructions:

1. Whisk together the potato starch, non-dairy milk, salt, and cinnamon.
2. Melt one tablespoon of vegan buttery spread in a frying pan over medium heat.
3. When the buttery spread is sizzling, dip a piece of bread into the batter, making sure the bread is coated on both sides. Place in the pan. Repeat, but don't crowd the pan.
4. After about 4-5 minutes, flip the bread.
5. Repeat with remaining batter and bread.
6. Top with maple syrup, berries or powdered sugar.

Apple Chips

Prep time: 10 minutes

Cooking time: 2 hours 30 minutes

Servings: 2

Suitable for: gluten-free, dairy-free, soy-free, egg-free, fish-free, shellfish-free, nut-free

Nutrients per serving:

Carbohydrates – 43 g

Fat – 0 g

Protein – 0 g

Calories – 163

Ingredients:

- 3 apples, cut into thin slices
- 1 Tablespoon coconut sugar
- ½ teaspoon cinnamon

Instructions:

1. Preheat oven to 225°F.
2. Put the apple slices on the cookie sheet.
3. Sprinkle coconut sugar and cinnamon on apple chips.
4. Bake for about 1 hour, flip slices, and bake for an additional hour (2 hours total).
5. Chips will continue to crisp up as they cool.

CONCLUSION

Thank you for reading this book and having the patience to try the recipes.

I do hope that you have had as much enjoyment reading and experimenting with the meals as I have had writing the book.

If you would like to leave a comment, you can do so at the Order section->Digital orders, in your account.

Stay safe and healthy!

Recipe Index

Conversion Tables

VOLUME EQUIVALENTS (LIQUID)

US STANDARD	US STANDARD (OUNCES)	METRIC
2 tablespoons	1 fl. oz.	30 mL
¼ cup	2 fl. oz.	60 mL
½ cup	4 fl. oz.	120 mL
1 cup	8 fl. oz.	240mL
1½ cups	12 fl. oz.	355 mL
2 cups or 1 pint	16 fl. oz.	475 mL
4 cups or 1 quart	32 fl. oz.	1 L
1 gallon	128 fl. oz.	4 L

OVEN TEMPERATURES

FAHRENHEIT (°F)	CELSIUS (°C) APPROXIMATE
250 °F	120 °C
300 °F	150 °C
325 °F	165 °C
350 °F	180 °C
375 °F	190 °C
400 °F	200 °C
425 °F	220 °C
450 °F	230 °C

VOLUME EQUIVALENTS (LIQUID)

US STANDARD	METRIC (APPROXIMATE)
1/8 teaspoon	0.5 mL
¼ teaspoon	1 mL
½ teaspoon	2 mL
2/3 teaspoon	4 mL
1 teaspoon	5 mL
1 tablespoon	15 mL
¼ cup	59 mL
1/3 cup	79 mL
½ cup	118 mL
2/3 cup	156 mL
¾ cup	177 mL
1 cup	235 mL
2 cups or 1 pint	475 mL
3 cups	700 mL
4 cups or 1 quart	1 L
½ gallon	2 L
1 gallon	4 L

WEIGHT EQUIVALENTS

US STANDARD	METRIC (APPROXIMATE)
½ ounce	15 g
1 ounce	30 g
2 ounces	60 g
4 ounces	115 g
8 ounces	225 g
12 ounces	340 g
16 ounces or 1 pound	455 g

Other Books by Tiffany Shelton

CPSIA information can be obtained
at www.ICGtesting.com
Printed in the USA
LVHW060929120322
713213LV00006B/229